BEAUTY AND WICKEDNESS

Beauty and Wickedness

A collection of poems
by
EDWARD V. BONNER

Adelaide Books
New York / Lisbon
2020

BEAUTY AND WICKEDNESS
A collection of poems
By Edward V. Bonner

Copyright © by Edward V. Bonner
Cover design © 2020 Adelaide Books

Published by Adelaide Books, New York / Lisbon
adelaidebooks.org
Editor-in-Chief
Stevan V. Nikolic

All rights reserved. No part of this book may be reproduced in any manner whatsoever without written permission from the author except in the case of brief quotations embodied in critical articles and reviews.

For any information, please address Adelaide Books
at info@adelaidebooks.org
or write to:
Adelaide Books
244 Fifth Ave. Suite D27
New York, NY, 10001

ISBN: 978-1-953510-23-5

Printed in the United States of America

Contents

The Corridor **11**

I Have Learned **14**

A True Gift **18**

A Woman and a Man **20**

Beauty and Wickedness **21**

Born of Sin **22**

All My Own (Hazelwood) **23**

Pain That Will Never Leave **26**

The Brilliance of Her Pomegranate Attire **28**

Torn **29**

Ebony Pearls **30**

Edward V. Bonner

Age of Aquarius *31*

Undiscovered Thoughts *34*

Encountered Souls *35*

Enticed *36*

Moment's Whisper *38*

Redeem My Soul *40*

Nature's Ghost *41*

Friendship *43*

Seasoned Wounds *44*

Engagement *46*

Hawaii *47*

Lucky *49*

Ravished Words *50*

Echoes in the Wind *53*

Uncovered Pain *54*

One Single Rose *55*

BEAUTY AND WICKEDNESS

Revealed **57**

Candlelight **58**

Words to Whispers **59**

Closer We Are **60**

Nature is Losing Her Battle **61**

Windless Charm **62**

The Devil's AR **63**

Obsession **64**

[What is Freedom] **65**

Life Quenches the Lips **67**

Voice of Drums **69**

A Dog from Hell **70**

Covered **72**

Happy Hour **73**

Gerti Schiele **75**

Raptured Bodies **77**

Edward V. Bonner

Far and Near-Simple and Clear **78**

Locked In Time **79**

Chasing Clouds **81**

The Ocean's Echo **82**

The Green Room **83**

Brilliance **85**

What's Your Muse **86**

A Poem **88**

Blossomed Thorn **89**

To Cathy **91**

Captive **93**

Decaying Leaves **95**

Opened Waters **97**

The Attic **98**

Between Life **100**

Between Dreams **101**

BEAUTY AND WICKEDNESS

Nature's Honor   ***102***

Society's Hell   ***103***

Masterpiece for Living   ***104***

Thoughts   ***105***

Waves of Change   ***107***

Atalia   ***108***

About the Author   ***139***

The Corridor

In regards to my own insanity'
I recollect having a talk with a young man.

Located perpendicular to the west wing.
Dark polished eucalyptus green.
Long narrow corridor from north to south'
heading to nowhere.

I recollect a windowless view
with rooms staggering
one by one across the corridor.

Eight by four heavy stainless doors,
with a peep to observe and guide.

This man we shall call "Mikey."
Mikey was a quiet person who walked all day
from north to south and south to north.

Mikey did not say a word.
He walked alone wearing slippers
and a blue one-piece jumper suit.

One evening I decided to talk to Mikey.
I started to walk with him.
We walked north to south and south to north.
This was the real "Rain Man".
Like an intense euphoric fusion.

You can guess my first question.
Why?
Why did Mikey walk
from north to south-south to north?
Answer:
"Stress, Anxiety, depression."
Mikey had a detachment with society.
And we walked.
Walked north to south-south to north.

My second question.
"What are the doctors going to do?"
"ECT" Mikey replied.

BEAUTY AND WICKEDNESS

"Oh, that's nice."
"What's ECT?"
"Electroconvulsive therapy,"
Shock treatment.
"Was Mikey's answer"

You got to be shitting me.
I murmured to myself.
"Do they really perform this procedure
"Yes". Mikey replied.
So we walked north to south-south to north.
I recollected shutting up.
But Mikey explained the procedure.

A couple days later'
Mikey was dressed in the sport coat,
dressed slacks and shiny shoes.
A smile from ear to ear

I Have Learned

I should have been dead half a dozen times.
Peaks and valleys
Consumed with pain, happiness
and a little disturbing history.
I've learned to survive.

Are there people worse?
"Of course"

With no father
my mother and I lived with my grandparents.
Freedom was more than most.

It all began when my second grade teacher announced,
"there wasn't a Santa Claus."
The fake jolly old man is now in my dead zone.
WTF

BEAUTY AND WICKEDNESS

A bus ride into Pittsburgh to see my mother working at
Kaufmann's department store.
"She was a hair stylist or as it was called "beautician."
A twenty-cent fare would take you everywhere.

Smoke filled skies.
Steel mills going strong
People by the thousands shopping.

First sight stepping off the bus
Hare Krishna dressed in gold gowns,
chanting with their brass percussion cymbals.
Bald headed girls!
I was clueless what the hell they were singing and never got
close.

April 4, 1968 hell broke out.
Martin Luther King was assassinated.
Riots began.
Firebombs bursting
Windows boarded up.
Schools closed.
An eight year old will never understand
the violence.
I was terrified.
Why was there so much hate?
A young man from God was murdered.
Peaceful and nonviolent
Martin Luther King was like a savior.

Discovering matches at 9 years old was a mistake.
During the riots I would soak a toilet paper-roll with
gasoline.
Light it.
Throw and run.

Then one day playing with matches
the woods behind my house became a seven alarm fire.
This accident ended my fascination with flames. Lucky no
homes were destroyed.

The scene of two ladies getting hit by a drunk driver:
one dead,
one screaming.
Their shoes knocked off.
Groceries covered the road.
Last, the drunk driver sitting in his car "dead" after hitting
a telephone pole.

Vietnam.
What more can I say.
Every day the death-count on the news
Visiting funerals and see these servicemen that fought in a
war I could never understand.
Why?

What I remember most
was my mother kissing me goodnight
all the joy in the world.

BEAUTY AND WICKEDNESS

My mother remarried.
My step father was the best dad anyone could have.
I've inhaled the good things in life.
I learned to strive and to set goals.
I am still street smart.

(1972 we moved to a suburb.
I saw the first freaking crow in my life.
Unbelievable.)

A True Gift

Gazing in the mirror
Reveals all the imperfections we hide
We apply an array of cosmetics to enhance attractiveness
Youthfulness
Sexual arousal
Temptation
All gives the human unequivocal excitement

Sculpted heads
Clay applied to flesh
A little polish for a mystic attitude

Movie stars
Politicians
Prostitutes
Our selves

The mind is a rainbow full of brilliance
From young to old
Men and women
Protect
Shield
Enshroud

BEAUTY AND WICKEDNESS

Social perception is created from evolution
Ancient Egyptians cover their bodies with dyes, perfumes
and ointment

Ageless on the outside is an everyday appearance
The word beauty fills our confidence
Confidence enhances prominence

Despite all this physical beauty,
"Inner beauty" is the true gift of love

A Woman and a Man

An immense light
Wrapped around his mortal soul
Standing in awe
Each coil propelled into his twilight eyes

In her voice
The vast pines serenade
Cascading nourishment through ethereal halos

Falling from her heart
A bough of fruit blossomed
Covering his naked body

The winds begin to howl
Clasping roots grow
Intoxicating
Harmonious
Ravenous (hips) bloom

A man and a woman
Makes love with the waves

Beauty and Wickedness

There was a place of beauty and wickedness
untouched from footsteps walking nowhere
Fixation drifting in the burning sun
turned the seas into a ravaged land

Bending the limits with the mind,
utters unique fantasies
Through inescapable happiness,
whispers plead for a utopian vision

A woman weeping in despair
retreats under a spellbound olive branch
Touched by this symbol of goodwill,
everyday life is an obstacle for learning

Move while the door is opened,
let resilience emerge from her sorrowful detachment

Fear can be clothed with excuses.
Return strength to the impeding heart
Recognize goals,
don't assume back tomorrow

Born of Sin

We all have been babies at one time
Black, white, yellow, red
Our skin was soft and delicate
But yet why does God let some babies have croup, scarlet fever, Reye's Syndrome and so on?
A child struck down to suffer

Born of a sinful state!
Why does God allow this to happen?
Creation to suffer for judgment on this planet!

Innocent suffering to enter the kingdom that belongs to our God
From all over the world children are stricken with agony.

Countries who know not of a God
Babies of the innocent

what is the measure for grace?
"A complex fallaciousness for humanity"

A simple answer doesn't relieve us at all.
Is free will always the answer?
"Born of sin"

All My Own (Hazelwood)

The morning sun peeped through my bedroom window
I remember when, oh wait! Mistaken for the morning sun,
a soaring flame of yellow, orange and red viewed miles away
hung in the sky all night and all day
Embodied a "plume of justice"
pride for the hard working souls earning a wage at Jones and
Laughlin steel in Hazelwood, Pittsburgh Pennsylvania

Living with my grandparents was great. But getting older, it
was time to move on

at eleven years old and remembering well
my mother and I moved into an apartment house, nestled on
a hill away from the town's confusion

in that, I acquired my first bedroom
a bed!

Edward V. Bonner

Wood frame, with a mattress and coverings
my first bed! Not a couch with sheets and a blanket
my first freaking bed!
I was in awe
my own dresser for clothes
Hot damn
I can store my army men in it
I'm one lucky kid

this was the greatest place!
Woods in the back of the house and a creek!!
Through the woods there was an old burnt up car
probably stolen and just past that car was the fishing hole
abundant with crayfish and lizards
Getting muddy and building forts with this child's
imagination,
was a world of heavenly dreams come true
Best of all, the city riots and fire-bombings were left behind

Yes, I threw rocks, bricks and one or two fuel lit amber
bottles
Retaliation is how we survived
There was no justice in the city
I was fast on my feet and often just narrowly escaped

We'd ride our bicycles below the tracks, about a mile away
Once there, we were safe in a community that protected us

The evening grew loud with trains carrying alloy of
iron and carbon

BEAUTY AND WICKEDNESS

"Steel" high stencil strength for building dreams

Damn!
It's late!
Time to ride home

Home with a bed and my own bedroom
What's more could I ask for?

Pain That Will Never Leave

As always a beautiful dusting of snow covering
the oaks and maples
But this day was going to be very distinctive

Upon the land of great wisdom, mortality affects each
individual on countless roads

Unraveling the eyes with terror, finds nowhere to escape
This heart continues to work through a rendition of character,
while a diminutive crowed gazes

"Can this literature be made out of agony?"
"For God's sake, my head is pounding."
"Wake me up from this nightmare"
But this was real and a gorgeous winter morning

BEAUTY AND WICKEDNESS

One hundred and twenty people commit suicide a day
I am watching the "one" of

She was seventy-two years old and alone
There was a risk
I should of acted

Now for the rest of my life, My mind sees this woman
gasping underwater

The Brilliance of Her Pomegranate Attire

The brilliance - of her - pomegranate attire
eddies a cologne - spiced opulence

Whimpers triggered - from a blazing blind - scarlet cloth,
curtains darkness behind a seductive temptress,
capable of impelling souls

Beneath her cocktail gown - silhouettes fire -
into radiating lust
Ravishing whirlpools impregnate warm currents
through his skin

Winds horseshoe vengefully - sending dynamite explosions -
across the sidewalk
Life turned to looming ashes

In that split-second change,
everything grew dark
Smudges blinded his delicate eyes beneath the clouds

Her hand went to his neck,
two punctures - seeped blood - continuously until death

Torn

The spirit weeps under candlelight.
Screaming and bleeding, revealed his torn body

Time was despairing to expel the hornet's venomous sting.
Acute pain continued beyond cogitable cohesion

Sweating like a drunken deserted derelict,
the concrete was his bitch
Fixated between the wheel and fender of a Volkswagen Bug
This was the lowest form in which Satan controlled his mind

Crimson braille
Night at the masquerade
It was a party with no face
Words that ignited flames into his scar
Rotting timber burned the lungs of young

Towering mountains partitioned
Nothing could be heard
He died for beauty
Unbeknown the truth

the stars held secrets
Love fell between seclusion and death
Questions cried
"Why did I fail"?

Ebony Pearls

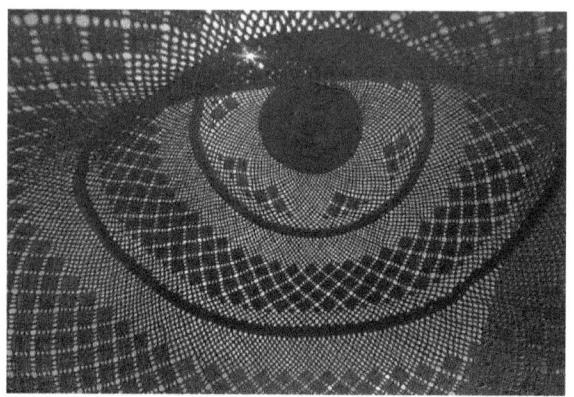

Upon her silent rapture
the eternal mind falls to flowered souls
endless purity devours the golden dawn
ebony pearls melt the hearts of forgotten love

Age of Aquarius

The cigarette fell twice from his lips onto the pavement
Right now the wind gusts are up to 20 miles per hour and
temperature 27 degrees

Yesterdays temperature was in the 60's with showers
just think if we can predict
would life be better?
Or would it be chaos?

We now know of an underground lake on Mars
Scientists have learned that the environmental conditions
where perfect for terrestrial microorganisms to survive
Will this be chaos?

Edward V. Bonner

The Poles are melting
water is rising
Chaos again

"Do I believe the monarch
or should I believe science?"

Truth may be harmful to society

DNA tests
the reality to reveal
Finding ancestors
and discovering our heritage

what we thought
Now we know
Is this a closure or a beginning?

Write to the President
"The new coming of age"
Aquarius again or is it the end?

Someday we'll be kissing the rats
Money will be paper to wipe our ass

Singing and laughing
Completely mad
Swiping flies with our tongues

BEAUTY AND WICKEDNESS

The "bomb" will not matter
Seven and a half billion people will be climbing the wall

The sky will turn upside down,
laughing in the face of humanity
Will there be enough toilet paper to go around?

One last drag and a flick to the ground

Undiscovered Thoughts

Perhaps to understand a pretentious statement,
depth will end in a reckless journey

Prophesies into the unknown will falter
with the smallest degree
At any rate,
the heaven's chosen is fate prior to conception

A warning to what you wish
Unpleasant consequences will erupt into a
hot flow of remorse

Souls of the unborn will haunt you
Life will become a madness
until your last breath is squeezed from your lungs

Encountered Souls

The streetlight shone on a man and a woman
Two bodies cast in form upon the walk

The snow fell light,
with feathered flakes twirling in the wind

Encountering souls where awakened from the shadows
There was never a sound, only the delicate breeze wrap
around humanity

The spirits danced in cadence from a tune of jubilant mortals.
Footprints brushed the ivory pavement
less the bodies figure.

Strangely
The fog will unfold this exhilarating gift
Seldom seen
are life's secret message.

As the couple part;
unbeknown,
only their prints are left in the snow.

"Captivating whispers,
capture serenity's embrace"

Enticed

Articulacy is outwardly silent
Penetrating the brain obscures intelligence

The violent storms brought out the viper in you
Dark skies, turbulent winds
embraced the cosmos

The wild
and your pink toenails.
Obsession followed your thighs
deep into nirvana

Everything was on fire
the will to burn
scorching erosion

The promises, the moments, our breath
softy assassinating
It's a beautiful psychosis welcoming tribulation
Everywhere around the moon stimulated the oceans
shifting the spectrum into brilliance

Inebriated from your Grey Goose-Red Bull
I was Tom Jones on stage

BEAUTY AND WICKEDNESS

"Salty sweat pores opened for love"
Incredible leather saturated all the way - down

The doors have been blown to pieces
what's to expect
For at least one moment rapture was sitting on edge

It's the nights that brought me here
Writing uncontrollable desires with my pen

Life is that much closer to Insanity or brilliance

"Imagine something greater than death"
A complex carousel
Around and around
Where fragments echo through bare hands
Spilling uncontrollably into space
again
around and around

Moment's Whisper

The morning sun glows deep in the forest
Glistening bodies stood silent,
awaiting their internal illusion to become will

Eloquent absorption speaks through mortal melodies
Moist desires are nestled with lavender spice

From a living essence she has awakened in a path of spring
A secret were the body has risen from dust to rose

Opened arms embraced the radiance of light
"Strange how her unfurled wings reflect a
chartreuse and turquoise glow."

I was a hunter with arrow nocked in bow
Speechless
I observed her natural splendor from a remote unsuspecting
plateau

a metamorphosis into godliness
my heartbeat rose like a fluttering butterfly,
emerging from her cocoon
yet my body was immobile and fixated upon her beauty

BEAUTY AND WICKEDNESS

"Can thought comprehend a miracle?"
This woman of elegant grace
turned to me a whispered
Then in a blink of an eye she was gone

"There are some things in life you will never reveal"

Redeem My Soul

Poison lilac leaves all the earth's blood redden eyes trembling
among the forest night

Searching through the burnt ash
Bones smoldering dust fog death
Hard blows and acidic love of young virginal women

Found are the scriptures
Possessed coveted power of Hell's
frontier

Oh Satan with your black plumage and metallic coloring
Give power to these lips that shall read
from the book of empty souls
Come strengthen these hands to power this land

Call what they are
Bark the secrets entwined in vain
Show the way

Reach inside my prison of invisible blood
Let it circulate through empty souls and give me power

Nature's Ghost

I am the god of wisdom
I live in the ancient forest that stood for thousands of years

With the crested moon horizon
Shadows emerge amid the countless leaves and limbs
Soon my time will embark on a journey of discovery
through the end

Silent wings will slice the darkness upon flight
When most of the world is asleep
I see the night come alive

The mouse
The rabbit and raccoon
Feed on clover, berries
Maybe some nuts and cherries

Edward V. Bonner

Hunger inside begins to overtake curiosity
I am the hunter
I reign in the cool dark woods

Bladed talons honed gracefully,
reveal a clean formidable weapon
A weapon for fresh living tissue
Piercing, cutting and ripping to shreds
Raw meat is best before bed

Swoop, dive and cartwheel
The forest is alive
Every rodent scurries to hide

Except
that one unsuspecting mammal which has full filled my hunger

This may be sad,
but it's God's way for us to survive

Friendship

You will never be alone
Our life was fate
I was always with you
My sweet friend thou our distance
is still
My heart follows you
Brave souls preserve guidance
through peace

Nourished spirits release deep,
clear and solemn healing
"I am her music,
where pure lips cast melodies upon the heavens"

Faith delivers fruit unto God without denial
"Let them see the path through our savior's hands"
Closing is the beginning of life

Serenity is prosperity
You will always be loved

Seasoned Wounds

I turned my head around and around
And everywhere I looked
There was life's restless frown

It has taken years to understand
But now the skies have closed to empty hands

Creatures are dimly observed in a society of concrete
Snowcapped mountains are diminishing at a pace too quick

Active volcanoes spew sulphuric dioxide
Exhaling molten magma into the beautiful seaside

Rocks, stones, windshields and cracks
Smoke filled acid provides your lungs with asthmatic attacks

Play
Provide
Piercing is lethargic
Leaving nature shattered in darkness

Till every season is tasted
The burning salt seeks wounds
Life of our forefathers are wasted
Like the unforgotten tomb

BEAUTY AND WICKEDNESS

Gabriel
My angel of everlasting faith
Come seek and heal this relentless wraith

Engagement

A trance
A solemn canvas night
There are no mountains
There are no meadows
Eternity is alone when you climb the ascending path

There is no day
Only the radiance of the stars without light
The moons are hidden
The spirits are in flight
Begotten the heaven's voice is a pulsating portal

For what life stood
Can you see your star
In this split second chance
Free yourself and deliver nourishment to your soul

Like lucid dreams
With its soft breath of quietness
This wisdom is awakened for absorbing enlightenment

Hawaii

Beggars play the boardwalk
Music to the ears of strangers
Captivating the ladies of the night

Japanese women stroll along
with their high heel fashion Gucci designers
Styling with their papa daddy
Six hundred ninety five suede pumps
Purchased in Paris

Where the wind whispers to reality
The beggar's mutt is tethered to a shopping cart
full of life's belongings

Cigarette stained fingers playing on his six string guitar
Many teeth missing,

Edward V. Bonner

But his smile is from ear to ear

Businesses cater to the wealthy
Prices are jacked-up
It's the rich they want
No matter what
Class is where it's at

The beggar
The pauper
The dancer
The player

Real to your eyes are the homeless

I offered money to a man sleeping on a bench
I startled him
He refused
Yes he refused

Behind him was a church
He was waiting for his meal for the day

Is this our world
My country
What have we done

Lucky

One drink
Maybe two
A martini
Dirty will do

A friend
Close to my heart
Kind that I can never part

Feelings may be hidden
Tenderness is internal
Life may not be easy
Our grace is held deeply

Numerous stumbles
But,
unpretentious charm
serving the soul
without any harm

In this short life that may be today
How lucky I am
To know you as a friend

Ravished Words

I'm standing in the doorway
Gazing in
My brave eyes have fallen
Only to be burned

They say it doesn't hurt,
but misery becomes a storm
ravishing the rainbow's smile

The skies and the butterflies were once magic
now the universe and the heavens weep
The summer morning passed
and the winter's bite is bleak

BEAUTY AND WICKEDNESS

The flamingos missed their turn,
ending in the Siberia domain
This dire soul needed love
only to be cast away

The sole lips, fleshy skin,
cracked from the toxic air

Still
I craved her moisture

once I held her hand
a woman
of mystic
Blameless mystery

how does bliss work?
Does it hover from the mind
of madness

Only now
I am the rotten,
worthless,
piece of scum
That fell on my knees

Yes I'm
Crying
Because I sacrificed life

Edward V. Bonner

In this, the arrow penetrates simple agony
Fruit will eventually be devoured by worms

Let this fall into nothing
Now that I know what was hidden
I might as well be dead

Echoes in the Wind

Basking the aromatic wilds
She slipped into a beautiful reverie befitting nature's theme

Galleries awaken whose stanzas are created
Inebriated bees renounce their sting

Shaping her mind from ignorant disputes
In itself
a single drop of dew reflects visions scribed into words

The wind draws the melodies working with the hand
Beyond the tongue spells themes like Romeo and Juliet
The Raven and Daffodils

Dispatch impossibilities
Let the door ajar
for what echoes in the mind

To her own
be patient
The brain is the sky
Let language summon infinity

Uncovered Pain

I held a jewel in my arms
And went to sleep
It was a day in March
Warm with love I'll keep

I was somebody
Or I felt to be somebody
I was a child in the garden of Eve
Brilliant amethyst held dreams and possibilities

However there was the Earth and a star
This uncanny distance retained ravishing enchantment for only the eyes afar

There is one further
Where only the moon will speak
It glows radiant with beauty until the blossoms peak

A piece of heart that spouts
unforgotten dreams
Is a taste
Two lovers forever sail—to fate

One Single Rose

If I could offer one single rose
with ruby petals,
blades of crimson,
showered in dreams,
from my garden where seasons are unknown
would you understand?

If a stream runs through graciously
In short,
under breath,
soft solemn covert sort
Would you understand?

T'wasn't far from my heart
and heard through the hills
The sky's inability to keep a secret cried to unveil

Edward V. Bonner

My falcon suspended alone in the clouds
Overheard the rumble
Gracefully retrieving the rose
He flew through the cascading summit,
protecting every petal not to crumble

This falcon possessed one single pure rosaceous plant

Whispered endearment to the one I love

in my life of reality
one single rose with ruby petals
one last breath with showered dreams
Ended from the whispering blows
of silence

Revealed

Yesterday's winter solstice was a silhouette in the sky
Where many portraits awake to come alive

Obsequious prophets awaited their call
From this quiet courtier
Time cannot erase
This unblemished love affair

Lord
Breath of breath
Seek the chosen
Divinity of the scriptures
Is finally revealed

Candlelight

Untouched by the blue hearts crystal,
where the alabaster clouds filter the sun's rays
Resurrected gale winds chill the morning breath

Summoned by mother,
nature awakens to partake
the joy of living

Ice crystals collide
Swirling and spiraling through the air
Each flake emerges
blending with the surfacing vapor

Life is gathered with each sip of wine
Wrapped in blanket
Divine pleasure the body will attend
under candlelight

Words to Whispers

To whom the sparrows sing
A breathless ballot they bring

Yet a heart that broke so long
His tender duty of resentment was wrong

Drowned in a woeful contusion
An unyielding confusion
Set beside in seclusion
Where life is a delusion

Remember him,
when rhythm screams
Intense passionate ardour
emanates a melodic energy of dreams

The voices in his head twisted loud
To no avail his seasons turned wild

He was a star, there was a star

Closer We Are

Everyday write a blessing about your life
Hold what's dear before departure
there's no formula for passion and preservation
a silent grace forgiving the wounds of many
will embrace wisdom internally

Nature is Losing Her Battle

To respect the simple days
Which carry the seasons by
We need dire direction
That is for you and I

To life's relevant existence
We simply must conserve
Each law forthcoming nature
Will be what we deserve

A florist full of roses
is a life the human perceives
But a forest full of acorns
Is God's food he leaves

Windless Charm

I did not surprise her
So she said or I thought
I fell to my knees
My question she forgot

Traveling athwart the forest
Crafted with jubilant sounds
Breathe in cottonwood and aspen
Love know not defiant bounds

Cooling the earth's atmosphere
The phantom meadow falls frost at night
Wingless angels petition songs
Calling for sacred rites

Today is far from infancy
Where we heard the woodland's spirit charm
Up and down the hills
I held her body in my arms

Yet, her eyes beheld what sacrifice perceives
Let the flowers bloom in the fadeless orchard
What's to remember
Only the windless departure

The Devil's AR

Piercing projectiles
burning the heart of innocent men
Core harden steel splits the body
like the devil's blade again and again

Here on this planet,
bloodshed drips beyond the sword
Through cement cracks,
the serpent's satin figure
slid stealthy following his whores

The tempest touched their garments
Lighting showered across their bodies
Horrid nightmares begin
As caskets lie in dark lobbies

Another shell ejects
Another life it takes
How many bullets can an AR shoot
All of them
From a mindless piece of scum

Obsession

He still believes
"Yet"
He's tormented by the obsessive passion that fell in despair
the hunter who remains in a silent prayer

[*What is Freedom*]

What is Freedom
Who controls individuality
What's your religion
Sensitized by narcissism
I am
I want
I'm jealous
What do you think
I want
I want
Me, me, me
What's my line

Freedom isn't free
It must be respected
Please go easy
Life is losing with time
Respect our world
Respect humanity
The sewers stink
Comb your hair

Confused driving in the rain,
wondering where life has gone
Only in America

Edward V. Bonner

Come on
Think
Tonight I know what you mean
The good
The bad
And the end
Greed will destroy society

Life Quenches the Lips

The chalice
The rim
The bowl
The stem
And are held under foot

The contours explode,
where there's no end
to drinking fine wine
as to the
sacred dark blue ink
encompassing her secret journey

Filling the vacuous space,
the mind is an invisible birth
enshrined through endless possibilities

As the violinist plays the chords,
the violin eventually wears down
and ceases to exist
But the music lives on
as words under glass fulfills
the heart with endless desire

Edward V. Bonner

Ageless wine never wakes up alone
It continues to thrive with ability
Language is ageless wine
ready to be awakened

Voice of Drums

My love
The day is nearly forgotten
The fall season has begun
Winds whip in a circular language,
nipping the waves of bitter silence

My love
Where did you go
Are you watching the leaf
that was a secret in the forest
slowly sculpting the ground

A voice drums in the night
soothing the imperfections
The truth is in your heart
Open the heavens
Allow the stars to enshroud our kiss

My love
My peace
My wild rose rooted to the soil
I will always wait
Bow in hand
Arrow fletched with multi colors

I am the earth and melody
that hymns call for love

A Dog from Hell

I don't know where to begin
But before I closed my eyes
I felt pain

Wandering through the shadows
with broken regrets
Each step the leaves crumbled
under my soles

My sleep will erase the fear within
Drifting graciously upon my soul
Delivering figments that once was

When the pitter of rain awakened
my dreams
The leaves which crumbled
turned into dust

What is now
Represents yesteryear
All those hands, eyes and feet
Expect nothing

BEAUTY AND WICKEDNESS

And yet society
can be a dog from hell

Later that evening
the children arrived
for a trick or treat

Covered

They traveled from place to place
only to dwell in the minds of a
macular fixation

Willing to answer challenges that are trapped beyond cryptic
messages,
a genius can live in a madhouse vomiting words after each
puff from a cigarette

Earth wonders
how the hell can humanity survive

Where degenerative images fade
and the tethered willows lay dormant
against the water's edge

Life sits at the end,
rocking in a chair
watching the hourglass spill
it's last grain into the bottom

Trapped until
the mental process
cartwheels into the lone abyss

Happy Hour

You don't know who I am
What's this all about
Two martinis
Dirty
With three olives

Watching all the people
It's happy hour
Time to enjoy
To get a buzz after work

Earlier today
I gave a homeless person
ten dollars
Was she on drugs
It doesn't matter

Her eyes broke my heart
Her smile made me cry
This beautiful young woman
thanked me and waved goodbye

How does a country with so much wealth
engage in so much poverty

Edward V. Bonner

Instinctive impulses are manifested into greed
and are beginning to overrun our society

Does anybody care

But yet
I look at myself in a bar drinking
Knowing I have a place to sleep

Gerti Schiele

A softened moon tastes the early sun
Dreams infused a creation
where young memories only begun

Eternal child,
reflections live with the stars of the universe
Let the radiance from her skin fill the canvas
with a silent thirst

Each stroke from his brush
encapsulated beauty
Compelled the obsessions
which eased a hidden duty

Adornment clothed
in silver and gold
Abstract minds laced
uncontrollably bold

Posing, exposing
Is this love
Is this fame
No one will ever explain

Edward V. Bonner

Was this abuse
For his special muse
Should we ever assume

Egon Schiele was a famous painter
His sister Gerti, was a graceful model

Raptured Bodies

Radiance sealed by fire
Enchanting winds
fell upon
raptured bodies

A slow autumn moon
crystallized the night's blade
Foliage caressing aromas
touched their tending journey

Down the spiraling peaks
Where they found each other's sweetness
Appeasing sounds weave with unbroken appetites

Let the wild become free
and Imbued with a golden spirit

Far and Near-Simple and Clear

I pray
I do not beg
To hear your voice
Before I'm dead

These words are clear
Deep in my heart
Simple and plain
To never part

My tears are dry
But my soul still weeps
A voice from an angel
Is all I seek

You cherish life
Don't be shy
Live to love
One last time

Know that I care
Far and near
You are that angel
I seek to hear

Locked In Time

Stargazing
Daydreaming at night
Musing at the universe's immensity
My thoughts of you
Soon take flight
In the vastness of a twinkling canopy

Where are you
Where are you now
I feel so close to you somehow
I feel you smiling down on me
Whispering to my soul
Blessedly

****

I am here
I have always been here
Waiting for that day
To carry your heart
I know we'll never part

Many moons and stars
Have gone by

Edward V. Bonner

Leaves have fallen
Our life is locked in time

The sun
The moon
Will go on

We are close to our end
I pray to God
We will meet in Heaven

Chasing Clouds

Looking into the past
I remember the days
When I was brave enough to love you
Climbed the walls to hold you
Chased the clouds to kiss you

Thoughts of days long gone
When love had just begun
You brought my young heart to life
Dreams dared to touch the sky

In twilight hours you were like a dove
With tranquility and grace I vowed to love
The infinite dreams that kept me alive
Each taste of your breath,
my heart would sigh

Looking into the past
Love was meant to last
Now lost in the memory of you
Climbed the walls of time to hold you
Chased the clouds to kiss you

Thank you Lucie Martin, my co-writer "Madame"

The Ocean's Echo

Stretched along the purplish arisen,
The Ocean speaks amidst the compelling wakes from above and below

Nostalgic worlds change with current,
grasping the magic seen only from dreams

Etched against the abyss,
her image graven
A deep echo,
freed from the bottom breaks,
surfacing in an amethyst glow

Amalgams of twirling waters become fervent,
Seething wine hues in a radiant sheen

beyond appearance
her image arose
sailing in an ethereal essence of life,
cultivating beauty for the Gods

Thanks to collaborator Lucie Martin

The Green Room

Wandering souls run ramped
in a foreign land

Heedless minds welcome a vaulted cage

Walking in circles
Waiting

Shock therapy
Rubber bite blocks
Gauze wrapped tongue blades

Coloring crayons and paper machete
engrossed his mind's attention

Read him poems
For he can't write or read
Pass them under the door

On his own
6:00 am
Breakfast, pills
Too late
He becomes irate

Edward V. Bonner

Read him another poem
Calming affect
Orderlies and police
walk him to the green room

Padded and a mattress
Alone

Brilliance

Blood soaked silk prowls the endless possibilities
Stretched canvas art runs through uncontrolled thoughts
widening the cornea of the eye

Piece by piece his tormented misery
speaks with a poetic gallery
Tint turns from a raven black vile
to a mosaic medley
Beading each color until vibrant hues
awaken the artistic masterpiece

Imagination is captured among glorious imperfections
What value of pain can be held with a brush in hand
Only from the mind of the creator

What's Your Muse

What you write, some people will corrode the
brilliant thoughts shaped from your mind

Close your eyes for one moment,
sense life's meaning into language
Spill your gut with compelling truth

"This is I" a shotgun in my pen
Scream over the black rose
The stem is thin and weak

You have a chance to breed
The bull's balls are in your hands
Be kind
Be original and creative
Hard words! Ha
Normal people want understanding
Laugh at what's makes you laugh
Cry at what makes you cry

You are the creator
Let your muse be discovered from natural ability
Look around
Dig deep

BEAUTY AND WICKEDNESS

Like a homeless person,
he seizes the opportunity to survive

Love, hate, society, be pissed off
We are all normal to a certain extent
The universe will carry what's left

A Poem

Alone is the ability to parallel uncanny thoughts to words
Silently disturbed or delightfully exciting

My illusion is your delusion, where haunting melodies glide
mysteriously to a conclusion

In our own words we cultivate meaning from thought
A physiological refuge unfolds the brain's secret vision
Time is eternity, but he who holds the key to freedom, holds
no boundaries for logic or reason

Open the windows
Breathe in
Invite the soul
Allow patience to manipulate your pen

Write a journal
Follow the journey
Start with reflection
Prosper from direction
End poem
Have a great day

Blossomed Thorn

Like a bud-less tree seeking sustenance in a fertile land for rain,

he pleaded for love
Found amongst the sheath,
thorns spewed out raw unheard of dialect

His story held meaning
Unbeknown,
the knot from her lace began to tighten
The bedroom began to spin
Vodka and Red Bull was his enemy
"A mixture eminent for destruction"

After a smoke
She returned
Upon this earth he vacated reason
They made love
The bedroom
The laughter
The dancing
"All a "FKN" mind playing game"
It was real to him
A getaway for her

Edward V. Bonner

Her circle was breaking free
His was caving in
Like a rapist on the street,
"hell" was coming early
Only he didn't know

Truly his love poems inspired what passion was left
Depth is hidden in the forest,
but the curvature of the earth is seen from space
Lying in bed,
the leaves turned dry and brittle
Everything turns to dirt
The drunken bee's sting!
Her earrings are left on the table
Spin to win
Feel her disease
it was only yesterday
Balance is somewhere
He believed

To Cathy

Screaming and scratching like the wild cats of Malaysia
a terrestrial bog filled her veins with enchanting pleasure

Tasting French wine and vanilla lips
A Chateau Moya flavored each kiss

Draw down the blinds
Test the poison
Clip the feathered wings

Let the eagle dance before his death

Symphonies play to the beggar
A timeless melody,
orchestrating a sonata form

Get the nails ready
Barricade the door
Kneel down before dawn

In this room,
hours of love

Edward V. Bonner

Sweat pouring
profusely

Drained from the memories
Piss on the shadows
I am dead

Captive

Without her smile
A choice of words
I'm falling forever

Turn out the lights
Until my soul breaks
Above the clouds
Far into the galaxy

Look past your dreams
Of hidden secrets
Unlock the door to the heavens

And if I don't breathe
There's nothing left to give

Pull away
Save yourself
I will wander alone

These wounds won't heal
Until the day
The moon surrenders to the earth

Edward V. Bonner

Lost into you
I'll fight away all the fear
I don't want to forget

Captive
You still have all of me
Take my breath
We'll be together again

Decaying Leaves

I miss the confusion
The meaning
Just as I knew misery
I sweat nervously gazing out the window

I see
Laying on a hedge
a mantis with her triangular head
and bulging eyes
praying with arms folded
waiting for a victim

Am I this victim
Where her smile feeds me
to stay alive

Arms wrapped around my waist
Unspoken, delicate, and on the edge
I cannot run away

Curse this feeling
To believe
What is there to believe
I have forgotten

Edward V. Bonner

But I keep going
And going

I love you
I hate you
I ignore the pain

The sun pans across the sky
Darkness sets in
I am a prisoner of decaying leaves
waiting for the moon to rise

Opened Waters

Seeking the endless fruit
in uncharted waters

Expelling my lungs
I excused life's identity
from the words of your mouth

my drunkenness for passion
was the pleasure of death

Trying to imagine
you with a tender breath

And when you are alone
Call me sometime
to hear the contentment
in my life
rain or shine

I hope ending up like you,
having life figured out

The Attic

Up the creaky stained dried attic stairs
Hidden words become a dreamer's delight

a single forty watt incandescent bulb emits
a three-dimensional shadow,
only the bravest human will investigate

Dust particles float between the sun's rays
and the dark abyss

Unpublished covert files,
tablets,
binders and literature,
a forgotten maker of reality

BEAUTY AND WICKEDNESS

Boxes full of things we might need,
pots and pans, antique glassware, clothing

Games like Monopoly, Parcheesi and Checkers
all waiting to come out of hibernation

even a good few strands of silk gathered spider webs hang
from the rafters
only to give us a miniature tantrum when they cling
to our face

Swatting, batting and slashing away the sticky goo
crying out the spider may be crawling on you.

Finally reaching the lone cedar chest
Positioned in the middle of the room

I see the past
I see the present
I see the future
"Everything is connected, all part of a whole"

Life is full of ups and downs for us to understand
Our choice is to follow or hide

Between Life

Because life matters
Not everything can be
the body begins to formulate an understanding where there
is no measurable distance between space

Becoming still,
Is there an indifference the mind will not travel
Counting is to understand a beginning,
where a lifestyle is to prosper from imagination

the stars that pass through the night are like an endless forest
hidden with creation

The womb of the universe
is the creation which leads' life to all that is

Love is the essence clothed in hands of enlightenment
"We shall live to face the spirit of existence"
What we understand about flesh
is what we are struck down with

"Now the stars bloom gorgeously away from our hand"

Between Dreams

I can't change who I am
I don't know where to begin

Gazing from the highest cliff
A beautiful dove called from afar
Her amber eyes blurred the
universe with endless passion

Between dreams
and reality
I breathed into her soul

When you said the words to me
You stole my heart
Happiness traveled beyond the oceans,
above the mountains and through the valleys
I could not resist the tenderness
that overwhelmed my fragile loneliness

A piece of my heart was stolen
leaving the arrow broken
As you slowly pulled
the remains out
I have bled till this day

Nature's Honor

The sun and the moon
venture to find their God wrapped around the wavering
clouds
Shadows appear across the Rocky Mountains

A faint howl is heard through the misty evergreens
Like a child reaching out from a deep slumber,
the wolf spirit calls to the souls of the past

Unyielding laws hover for survival,
yet his poetic love calms his ferocious path with society

Save the code
Invite life and
honor her beauty

I am you
We are one

Society's Hell

She crawled from pain
that society delivered
Reaching out,
a visitor heard her cry

this woman of silence,
is a warrior in life

A mother of selfless courage,
lived with commitment and no guarantees

"A poor white woman living in hell"
What applies to society's make up?

It takes a lot to know
it takes a lot to understand
to look back

Effects are far beyond a remedy
a heartbeat from hell

is there a way out?
Unbeknown
But yet
Pain is what experiences
made her today

Masterpiece for Living

Without words, depth conceives magic
Igniting power we encourage victory above the horizon

Peace is the splendor of elegant smiles
He who binds the earth from joy,
spreads pain to their soul

However, laughing needs but little
Perhaps an honorable thought of compassion or gratitude

Funny is funny
Laughter expresses a portrait to every human personality
It will cross boundaries that separate people
A spontaneous uncontrollable emotion, randomly
unexpected thoughts like capturing a blooming daffodil
Cause and affect

Where there's nothing to give,
laughter opens doors to a symphony of chords
A simple masterpiece promoting creativity to the minds of
the young and old

Day or night, when it's raining or bright
Giggles
Smiles and explosive roars
This art we carry embraces scores

Thoughts

Enjoying the glorious flame
which moves with egotistical manifestation

Life wraps around a shell
in the depths swallowed by sea

What is seen in the mirror
reveals an isolated human being

We are driven by fear from society's force

Look beyond the image
and seek to humble yourself

A blind child learns to conquer obstacles
by touch, smell and sound

Beyond the flame
there is life
without torment

The "way" captures
development in one's self

Edward V. Bonner

Cultivate spiritual respect
is a reward
for harmonious methodology
Thus creating a paradigm
through thought

Waves of Change

Goodnight my darling
till the sun begins to rise
I reach for you each morning
before dawn of the crimson sky

A kiss on the eyes
A kiss on the lips
Until we're aware of the heat
we can't resist

When I lay with you
I thought I knew
But I can feel your heart cry
Let the dark fall
for what is believed
and let the winds carry us by

See the difference
between chaos and love
around your soul
Let the moon cross our path
a truth that we may hold

Thanks to collaborator Judeen Wayman

Atalia

Across Asia to Turkey
through Pakistan and Burma

Beyond the poppy fields
inhabits a small town of peasants.
Mountains held this secret in the shadow's frost.

Perfect surrounds;
conceal the "lords" beyond visualization.
Death in this dream becomes reality.

Blistered and stained hands.
Fingers are digging.
"Cultivating opium
from seed to sale,"
petals fall from the flower,
they become pods.
These pods are squeezed until the sap is extracted, pressed
into bricks, wrapped and sold to dealers.
Morphine is then extracted from the opium sap by way of
boiling water and lime
to process heroin.
Dangerous chemicals are mixed with morphine and boiled

producing a white powder.
Unbeknown, a kiss from Satan:
Heroin!
Because many peasants are addicted to opium,
the infant mortality rate is disgraceful.

Lost in her paradise,
is a farm girl dressed in
shabby burlap garments.
Deer hides sewn together
for shoes; protect her young fragile feet
from fire ants.
One single sting
will cause intense pain for days.

"Love cannot be seen in the poppy fields among the working people."
"Time is the essence to harvest their livelihood."
The illicit crops are hidden between corn rows, amongst rice, beans and sugarcane.
Moreover, freedom rights are suppressed among the peasantry.

Her name is Atalia.
Meaning: "God is great"
"A spunky 9 year old with long dark hair, olive skin, hazel eyes and a brilliant smile"

Atalia had an art of gaining wisdom from her parents.
She had her own ideas for living,
to endure knowledge to the most capacious state.

Suffering was a general onslaught among the natives,
merely because the drug cartel engaged in embezzlement schemes, intimidation and murder.
"That of which influenced the government officials to hide."

BEAUTY AND WICKEDNESS

Other than working the fields,
Atalia's favorite pastime was investigating nature.

Ten thousand-thousand butterflies spread their wings.
The mouse-deer roam the dense foliage in the forest.
The Crested Partridge with its stunning plumage is seen
feasting on nuts and berries.
Many unique birds sing in unison.
This inspiration covets Atalia's vision to escape.

Late at night,
Atalia studied the stars in splendor.
Tethered with no wings,
   she was spellbound.

"Heroin" the seed capital of Burma, spirits the economy.
Lo Hsing Han, the Burmese drug lord, trafficker and
business Tycoon "owned" the country.

For years,
Atalia's parents, Nan (mother's name) and Zaw (father) saved
every kyat (ch-yat) currency for that one day to escape.
"A life savings for freedom or death."

The Lingaya youth anti-drug organizational group consisting
of students against the cartel were called to rescue.

For the family to escape,
they will need assistance
from an internal link.
One standing soldier patrolling the fields is their connection.
Two thousand kyat persuaded the guard on duty.
"Roughly one dollar and thirty cents, U.S. money."

  Time:
"Twenty three hundred hours."
The cartel soldiers will be gambling and drinking.

BEAUTY AND WICKEDNESS

Zaw, Nan and Atalia gather the most important essentials.
The trek on foot takes 5 days from Taunnggi Mountains to
the port of Rangoon.

The moon-drawn grave with the unforgettable cries are heard
bellowing a death crumbling innocence.
Flesh of a naked corpse foaming marrow through his
splintered bones lay as a warning to the people if they try to
escape.

The guard "Sa'ir" guides the family through a clear corridor
in the jungle.
Snares, punji sticks are sharpened, heated and deployed in
substantial numbers.
Life's uncut rule is a journey.
Only few know the path to safety.

Nearing the end of the perimeter, their pulse spikes,
the last corpse hanging:
A warning to all that enter or flee will end in death.

If not killed, many are subjected to human trafficking.
Forced labor and forced prostitution
are widespread.

A farewell from the guard,
the family of three is on their own until they meet with
Lingaya youth organization.

When freedom—opens wide the gates—instinct will take

flight,
searing the sky with propelled energy.
Of men and creatures, the brain responds to salvation.
Faith is the divinity from the devil's hands.

Returning to the compound
Sa'ir was overtaken by the drug lord Lo Hsing Han.
With no regards, the cartel members preformed a public execution
dismembering Sa'ir in front of his family.
Removed his eyes and thrown to the pigs.
Later, they hung his body at the edge of the compound next to the other soul that lost his life.
Is a warning to all that render assistance.

Visionary thoughts of heaven,
or haven,
the family tread through the jungle unknowingly for what's to come.
There is a jarring on the nerves yet no outbreak.
Will there be peace at the end?

The wind whips the wrong direction,
trees point up and down.
Suddenly wild dogs are heard howling.
The mind plays tricks.
Clouds roll wickedly over the mountain's peak.
"Is this the devil's tongue,
or the Trinity's embryo?"

The family scurries to find cover.
An old canvas tarp that Zaw carried was placed carefully over limbs from a Tsuga dumosa, commonly called a Himalayan hemlock.

Slowly raindrops begin.
In wait for this tropical storm,
Atalia, Nan and Zaw embrace under the canopy feeling each other's heartbeat.

Weather from flesh and bone drives darkness to light.
Lighting illuminates the internal sky.
The eye of the womb erupts in the tangled land.

Water slowly seeps through the canvas tarp.
Each drop falls on Atalia's neck making her uncomfortable.
Letting go this annoying feeling'
her intuitive mind
concentrates on freedom.

After the demented storm'
a calm and strange beginning silhouette's the morning rise.
Gray shadows come alive.
Are these ghosts unearthing the jungle?

In delight the valley awakens with a small covey of Asian Blue quail bursting into high pitch sounds, low chuckles or grunts like a lost pig. Flapping of wings removes excess water, keeping the feathers oiled well.

Up early.
Nan prepares breakfast.
A little rice and greens mixed with spices, and then placed on flatbread.
The smell sparks Atalia under her father's arms.
Atalia nudges Zaw to rise.
The family must eat quickly in order to meet up with the Lingaya youth group.
The hike is approximately seven hours to the town of He Hoe.
This is where the convoy will be waiting.
However, Lo Hsing Han is aggressively pursuing to capture.

Lo Hsing Han's number one priority is money and control.
Lo and his son, were the military's most powerful business associates and were awarded contracts to build roads and seaports.
His persistent demand reigned supreme power over the country.
His militia consisted of three thousand men and women guarding his opium.

With Lo's order,
six militia men were ordered to pursue and prosecute the escapees.

Atalia's parents decided an alternate route to He Hoe.
They would travel south through the town Char Thar, following a deep descent south-east.
Next was the switchback-trail leading up the ravine past a Buddhist temple known as the "pure land."

Burma was part of the Golden Triangle.
The country was one of the highest producers in opium.
Zaw, Nan and Atalia were to travel through history
"the most extensive drug route in Asia."

For Atalia's family, the power of hope harmonized with conviction, replenishes the soul under intense conditions.
"Walking dreams are a hunger for living."

In a solemn manner the three stood listening to the wind. Nothing was said.

Approaching the top of the switchback, Zaw spotted a
reflective figure at the bottom of the ravine.
The cartel soldiers were gaining rapidly.

With memory and the measure of death'
"Will this family be captured, dismembered,
suspended,
while pigs devour their eyes?"

Atalia started to sob.
Is there hope?
She whispered to her mother.
Nan explained. "The shining surface of a pond is all we see,
look beyond the water, and look into the depths of the future.
Something more is hidden, a gift from God?
Life is to live.
Live is to survive.

There is but one thought,
the peasants have suffered from
the Earth's savagery.

A light shower begins,
inadvertently slowing down the cartel soldiers on the
switchback mountain.
The trail becomes treacherous.
Zaw is relieved, knowing how rain mixed with clay becomes ice.
The soldiers will lose ground.
Having approximately three and a half hours to reach He Hoe;
the trek will be quick and easy for the family.

Fingers sunk deep into the mud.
Vigorously proceeding in a careful manner:
Each cartel member screams and claws to gain footing.
Instantly the first soldier slips,
plunging three hundred feet against the jagged rocks.
His skull is quickly cracked and shredded into pieces.
Limbs flutter like a rag doll to the end.

Crying, screaming, the men are a burden to the mountain.
Evil opens his ponderous gate.
Digging desperately:
Their fingernails separate from the skin.
Grotesque vessels form on their face.
Violent tremors seize the mind.
One last grasp, they fall into the broth of Satan's soup.
Never to be seen again.

Upon the unparalleled light, it's impossible for Atalia to conceive
this unexpected life of freedom.
Nine years growing up in a brutal
atmosphere was a convulse madness.
Yet she conceived beauty from nature.

Next to the railway, behind the He Hoe market,
Aug Moe Way and the Lingaya Youth group met each family member.
Many factors come into play when Atalia, Nan and Zaw appeared.
Actual garments and moccasins were handed to the family.
Fixated on the three escapes,
the filthy burlap rags draped over their bodies were removed.
Standing while being cleansed, they (the family) were
unaware of the word "nakedness."

After a day's rest, the hike commenced.
They must travel through the Mandalay jungle.
It will take approximately twenty four hours to cross.
Many of the most endangered creatures live in this range.
Tigers, Burmese Pythons, Snub-Nose Monkeys and the most recognized animal, the "Great White Elephant."
White elephants are regarded as symbols of power and fertility.

The internal joy is but a small glow from the North Star.
What can be predictable is unpredictable.
Let it break from the world's wound and the bloodshed turn an eye.
For all men that adore God must pray and the wicked will milk Satan's breast.

BEAUTY AND WICKEDNESS

Beyond the mist-shrouded jungle:
Nature remains isolated in a timeless land.
Combining the ancient Buddhist monasteries with the natural landscape,
Atalia and her parents were
mesmerized from this unspoiled utopia.

Not long after, the Lingaya group discovered an enormous cave concealed on the mountain's edge.
The cave's interior was decorated with breathtaking murals and a vast collection of Buddhist statues.

Buddhism is twenty five hundred years old.
The religion provides the teachings through suffering and the need to expel.
"A process to achieve enlightenment."

If Atalia felt any emotion at all, she prayed at the clever display in extricating oneself from pain accumulated in the channels of her mind.
At the end, Atalia saw nothing but the stars, the sky
and the moon, which had arisen.
A full tropic radiance appeared to her innocent eyes.

The Lingaya group decided that everyone will stay the night.
Rest is crucial for the long journey to freedom.

At night among the shadows of the trees and the brush, there exists a very active world.
Nocturnal animals are roaming the darkness.
Bats with their skin webbed wings provide astonishing entertainment.
Diving, screeching, acrobatic maneuvers feeding on gnats, mice and mosquitoes:
Most bats hunt using echolocation sound waves bouncing off objects to navigate.
An Asiatic Black Bear is seen foraging high in the trees, eating nuts, berries and insects.
Atalia noticed the remarkable black coat of fur, and a distinctive white V-shape marking on his chest.
"What great beauty for her to observe,
   tomorrow will be a new day."

Atalia found herself awakened from a confused and terrifying dream.
It was now midnight, no definite comprehension.
Yet this memory has revealed horror.
A page from her previous existence;
the young were sold to the seafood industry's underworld.
It's a brutal trade that has operated for decades as an open secret in Southeast Asia's waters.
Corrupt companies rely on slaves to supply fish to markets and stores worldwide.
The Burmese people were trapped and beaten aboard a floating prison.
Girls were kidnapped and sold for prostitution or sex slaves.
The world is half the Devil's.
"A nightmare borne within reality."

Atalia's mother comforted her.
Nan whispered to Atalia saying,
"remove the obstacles in your journey, adapt to honor righteousness,
much like the atmosphere of the earth."
Under the star covered skies, they prayed until asleep.

The sound of thunder shatters everyone sleeping.
However, it's not a thunderous storm.
It's a poacher shooting off his M16 rifle,
killing everything in his way.
"Professional poachers are known to operate in Burma, particularly along the Karen Hills. With many endangered species, it is a supreme hunting ground for those feeding China's high demand for exotic animals."
Armed gangs under the control of the drug lord Sai Lin are getting involved in the animal trade. These gangs stretch across Burma and through China.
If the market continues, the remaining wild animals will slowly be extinct.

Atalia and her family hid deep into the cave. The Lingaya group covered the entrance to the cave with vines hanging from the hillside.
With only two SKS rifles in arms, they prepared for the worst.
Heart pounding;
Sweat pouring;
Cadaverous species fall thick and steady.
Without the sun or the stars they wait for the poachers to pass.

Each chimed bullet echoes like a hangman's scream.
Splitting the ears with a bloodied death moan;
gunpowder permeates the air, traveling downwind through the arterial nerves.
This becomes a war zone to God's creatures.
Time in the hour-less cave shaking:
From Adam's grave, man has scaled his skull on his trophy mantle.

After a few hours the carnage ceased.
Fortunately,
Atalia only witnessed the sounds and smell from the slaughter of animals.
What her brain absorbed, visualized senseless killings for greed.
Death is a metaphor encompassing the shape of destruction.
This innocent child and many others are sucked into the planet's artery nestled against its aneurysmatic wall.

Exiting the cave,
mixed with jungle plants and blood, a metallic sweet yet
horrid smell permeated the air.
Entrails scattered on limbs, in streams and all over the land.
A slaughterhouse in the opened
wilderness, hidden from world'
the forest has gone silent.
Dead is beyond dead.
Atalia cannot understand the reasoning behind this
destruction, only the pain felt in her heart.

Traveling through the jungle, the family encountered a
variety of ethnic tribes.
One group in particular captivated Atilia's enthusiasm.

The Kayan tribe or the "Long Neck People."
What was unique about these people, the women would wear
brass coils around their neck.
These neck rings appeared to lengthen the neck; however the
weight of the brass rings pushed down the collarbone and
compresses the rib cage.
Many origins surrounded this custom.
It was said the coils were to protect their neck from tiger
bites.
Another is the sign of beauty to attract a husband.

Dressed in multi colors the Kayan villagers were slightly
skeptical.
Their children hid behind bamboo trees, peering out at the
strangers.

Don't be fearful little ones.
The gentle children began playing;
God; their fate got lucky.

A tall well aged man with tattoos on his face appeared to the escapees.
He welcomed them as the stars twinkle in the night sky.
His name was "Nyan," meaning "Wisdom."
A brilliant power embodied all characteristics of a leader.

There was glory to hear from its lost wilderness.
Peace was the earth.

Nyan invited Nan's family and
Aung Moe Way into his home.
Nyan's home was made of wood and leaves; there was no electricity or proper sanitation.
Nyan's wife "Therein" meaning "The Sun" fed everyone rice and greens.
Filling their bellies, Nan explained his family's escape and how the Lingaya youth group is helping their cause.

After eating, Nyan entertained the family playing his hollow guitar.
Atalia danced to music for the first time in her life. "A taste of freedom and joy."

Edward V. Bonner

A blade of grass cries for a meadow,
a frog naps in a puddle of mud.
Open the clouds for the innocent to grow.
She alone lies waiting,
between man's corruptions.

Last night with unlocked moons,
Atalia's arms opened with luminous charm.

The family stayed overnight;
first time in a dry four walled grass roof building since their escape.

Lonehkwone Saw, "safe" in Burmese language.
A word unknown to slaves'
How precious is this word we take for granted?

The morning drank the wind, free and fast.
With tremendous thanks,
Good-bye to the Kayan family.

Following the Lingaya youth group,
one by one Zaw clings to the hands of Nan and Atalia.
Blinded eyes, sting on lips,
insects echo across their face.
They walked the earth through a time-tunnel absorbing life.

The passage through the jungle was getting more feasible.
Meadows could be seen surrounding a boundless waterway.
The group arrived in the village of Yenzin.
A small up and coming village for agriculture'
However, life in the area was very hard and took a heavy toll for families to survive.

While the Lingaya group went for supplies,
Zaw, Nan and Atalia stayed hidden in the outskirts for fear of being apprehended and sent back to the cartel.

A crystal clear stream in the area made it enticing for the family to wash.
Atalia loved lying in the water and having it flow through her hair.
"To be clean is an experience we take for granted."
Atalia realized how lucky she was, and then cried.
Cried for the people that live like slaves'
"At one time seventy five percent of Burma's population lived in poverty."

Guided by a bare-footed farmer,
a large, dark onyx colored ox is spotted pulling a plow through the rice fields.
"What is the side of truth from the eyes of the innocent?"
Forgive which is evil.
Drown the darkness beyond the cock crow.
In this hollow romantic image, survival is a human instinct.

Under virtually all conditions, Burma is a living laboratory for practically every disease.
Over five million rats alone in the village of Rangoon. What logically unfolds is roughly sixty-five tons of rat feces every year.
Bubonic plague, known as Black Death killed thousands.
Drug resistant malaria, tuberculosis and others are among the highest in the country.

After a five hour wait, the Lingaya group returned with enough supplies for what seemed to be an endless escape.
Rice, vegetables and fruit were handed to the family.
Atalia ate well that evening.

Early morning was after the blackest shade opening for the sun.
A peaceful gloom wreathed a silhouette from each tree.
Pleasure is still within reach.
In truth, man must behold the glory of God.

There next passage forthcoming will trek south from Yenzin to Thar Ga Ya. The walk is approximately thirteen hours through small towns hoarding rebellious tribes.
Traveling south, they'll parallel the Pyinmana Myo Shaung Road walking in many rice and bean fields.
Many reasons traveling off road, not to be noticed by the locals and the corrupt military.

Green spheres that meet the dusty roads, rough as the sun's core beats down on their feeble bodies.
Tongues thrashed with brambles for rain.

Atalia's tears were like petals from a rose, drifting magically with the wind.
Sad and beautiful, she will never abandon her dream.

The family embarked from the depths of the rice fields.
A slight heat wave across their skin drifted as they walked across the food plots.

Moving forward they rushed passed the military base in the village of Yaw Ni.
Both Nan and Atalia disguised to look like males.
Being seen as a woman they may end up raped or murdered.
With so much corruption in the military, the family never stopped moving.

The Burmese government was a subnormal entity, exploiting people.
Many ethnic tribes were tortured because of certain beliefs.
Some radical leaders used their authority to mistreat the poor.

"Solders abused drugs and alcohol.
Degraded humanity, created a virus within society.
Beatings were an everyday occurrence."

Despite the many obstacles,
their surge continues for a true living democracy.
Resilience is what will be embedded into Atalia's mind.
Zaw and Nan provide the ability to see failure and to
overcome its disadvantages. Atalia is not the outlaw, but the
proprietor for a new beginning.
Through learning and responsive action she is the
constellation to wisdom.
"The truth is to seek within."

Arriving in village of Lewe, Atalia can see a Buddhist temple
perched high along the mountainside.
The holy site features a stone brick central tower standing
at about one hundred feet high, as well as four smaller ones
surrounding it. The Stupa embodies several shrines and
statues outside the main tower depicting Buddha's life.
Unique features of this temple were spellbound.
Unlike the present day structure of gold leaf and plated
exterior,
garlands, flames from the sun, peacock tail feathers and
mythical creatures were embedded into this ancient structure.

To the west of the compound sat a Burmese nunnery.
Children as young as five live at the monastery.
"Many girls become nuns because they have a problem—no money, no family, protection from abuse and slavery."

Dressed in pink bamboo-cotton robs, red harem pants and shaved heads.
Buddhist Nuns have taken monastic vows and are called "Thilashin," meaning owner and protector of virtue and ethics.
This oasis undisturbed, is dedicating their lives to learning and teaching Buddha.
Yet these women are not equal to their male counterparts.
They are considered a lesser individual (laywomen) to the monks.

In this existence,
you are the fountain of life.
From a child's heart,
Atalia's vision is a divine path aiming for purpose.
Some people marvel at the harvest but not the seed.
Atalia is the seed to develop growth in equality.

In great need, the family asks for "Food rations and water."
Daw Aye Thada (senior nun and provider) invited Atalia and her parents into compound.
The Lingaya group gave their respects through almsgiving,
Thus developing a spiritual realm for humbleness and humanity.

This meeting in itself, wasn't merely for supplies.
Atalia is in a precarious position, constantly in danger of slave trafficking.
Daw Aye counseled the family about Atalia's safety.
"Thousands of girls were being sold each year from Burma to brothels alone."

The nunnery would be a safe haven for this precious girl.
Education is the nunnery's primary concern.
At age eighteen, the girls will decide if they want to stay or leave to look for a new life in the country.

A decision if made, Nan and Zaw may never see Atalia again.

How to be the thinnest crescent moon, there was no choice.
Atalia will continue with her mother and father.
The stars will be watching over them and guide with inner love,
from their savior.

With prayers from the Daw Aye, the group commences on their journey to freedom.
The final trek to Rangoon will take two days without any obstruction.

On the trail heading to Rangoon they met up with the anti-drug group called "Pat Jasan."
Pat Jasan is a Christian organization working to destroy poppy fields all through Burma.

Tan Joon, head of Pat Jasan provided the family with a Jeep and driver.
As a result, the two day walk develops into a four hour drive to Rangoon.

The eyes of a stranger stare into the abyss.
Their rope liberated life to breathe the mysteries through love.

Traveling in silence with integrity; moving forward as if fighting your way out of a robin's egg.
It isn't easy.
First the baby chick must break the shell, then struggles with all its might to freedom.
Naked and unaware, life becomes a challenge for survival.
The chick is helped by the adults until flight.

Behind the sufferings reveals beauty.
A path where light shines in the darkness and darkness explodes into fragmented crystals. Atalia is learning the skills to conquer. What was merely thought is now fortune upon her quest.

The family arrived in Rangoon at
two-hundred hrs. (Two a.m.)
The last and final excursion with the Lingaya group was a small ferry down the Rangoon river to the Andaman sea.

Arriving at the port was nothing but chaos.
A wave of strikes hit Rangoon and elsewhere in the country against a backdrop of corruption, inflation and food shortages.
Troops opened fire on the workers at the dock yards and railways.

From this immense attack, Atalia was separated from her mother and father.
Aung Moe stayed with Atalia.
The firing of rifles was getting closer to the people.

BEAUTY AND WICKEDNESS

Aung Moe found a freighter departing at the harbor.
Sprinting to the entrance, Aung Moe bribed a shipmate to
allow Atalia become a stowaway from this unforgotten place.

The last glimpse Atalia had of her parents; was disappearing
in the crowd.
What is known to be unknown is more painful than
understanding awareness.
Will Atalia see her mother and father again?

The young sailor fed Atalia on the long voyage. Not knowing
where she was headed. Atalia asked the sailor. "Where are we
going?"
The sailor said. "Look up at the flagpole, what do you see?"
Atalia: "A flag with Stars and Stripes, what does that mean?"
The sailor responded: "Freedom."
Fifteen years later on August 8, 1988. "Called 8888
uprising",
a nationwide strike involving thousands of students,
Buddhist monks and ordinary citizens led protests across
Burma, calling for a true democracy and an end to military
rule.

Troops began firing into the crowd killing over 3,000 people.
While many of the citizens fled, some protesters stayed and
fought back with fire bombs, swords and even poison darts.

The soldiers were so ruthless; they killed doctors and nurses
treating the wounded at the Rangoon hospital.
Many student leaders were sent to jail for years to come.

Not one government official was prosecuted for the slaughter of innocent people.

In 1988 the military rule changed the name of Burma to Myanmar.
In 2011 Rangoon became Yangon.

As for the "Pat Jasen" anti-drug group,
many were ambushed by local farmers and drug lords.
Some were shot, and beaten with sticks.
The group has decided to abandon their campaign.

As for Atalia, she is a grown woman living in a free world.
God bless you.

About the Author

The titles of **Edward V. Bonner's** poetry, suggests some ways in which the poems inside balance the universe. Most of the poems examine the themes of beauty and risk, pleasure and danger, in the context of one of three kinds of relationships: to romantic partners, to the spiritual world, and to the world of nature. But while these concerns are shared by much of humanity, Bonner's poems sound consistently personal.

As a young child, Ed grew up in a rough area of Pittsburgh Pennsylvania, a small mill town called Hazelwood. Raised by his mother and grandparents until the age of 13. (As Edward Fromen) His mother remarried. At 15 years old he was adopted by his stepfather.

Growing up Bonner got into trouble like most city kids. Only he was the lucky one.

An avid outdoorsman

6^{Th} degree black belt in Shotokan karate

Holds a degree in business

Holds aeronautics degree and an A&P license. Employed at American Airlines/Usairways

Each poem is carefully chosen to serve the reader.

Author of "One Kiss- Just One Kiss"

Author of "Through the Eyes of a Lost Boy"

Published in "Adelaide" literary magazine (Purple Dawn- poem) Year III Number 11, January 2018.

Published in "Adelaide" literary magazine (Beyond the Heavens) Year III Number14, July 2018.

Finalist: ADELAIDE VOICES LITERARY CONTEST 2018 "Verdant Whisper".

ADELAIDE LITERARY AWARD: ANTHOLOGY 2018

SHORT LIST WINNER "THE ATTIC"

LATE NIGHT POETS ANTHOLOGY VOL. 1

"AUTUMN PEAK" PEN NAME –EDHUNTER

LATE NIGHT POETS ANTHOLOGY VOL. 2

"PANTHER CREEK" –EDHUNTER

www.ingramcontent.com/pod-product-compliance
Lightning Source LLC
Chambersburg PA
CBHW032231080426
42735CB00008B/802